The 21 Golden Rules for Cosmic Ordering

The 21 Golden Rules for Cosmic Ordering

HAY HOUSE

Australia • Canada • Hong Kong • India
South Africa • United Kingdom • United States

First published and distributed in the United Kingdom by:
Hay House UK Ltd, 292B Kensal Rd, London W10 5BE. Tel.: (44) 20 8962 1230;
Fax: (44) 20 8962 1239. www.hayhouse.co.uk

Published and distributed in the United States of America by:
Hay House, Inc., PO Box 5100, Carlsbad, CA 92018-5100. Tel.: (1) 760 431 7695
or (800) 654 5126; Fax: (1) 760 431 6948 or (800) 650 5115.
www.hayhouse.com

Published and distributed in Australia by:
Hay House Australia Ltd, 18/36 Ralph St, Alexandria NSW 2015.
Tel.: (61) 2 9669 4299; Fax: (61) 2 9669 4144. www.hayhouse.com.au

Published and distributed in the Republic of South Africa by:
Hay House SA (Pty), Ltd, PO Box 990, Witkoppen 2068.
Tel./Fax: (27) 11 467 8904. www.hayhouse.co.za

Published and distributed in India by:
Hay House Publishers India, Muskaan Complex, Plot No.3, B-2, Vasant Kunj,
New Delhi – 110 070. Tel.: (91) 11 4176 1620; Fax: (91) 11 4176 1630.
www.hayhouse.co.in

Distributed in Canada by:
Raincoast, 9050 Shaughnessy St, Vancouver, BC V6P 6E5.
Tel.: (1) 604 323 7100; Fax: (1) 604 323 2600

A catalogue record for this book is available from the British Library.

Previously published in German by Ullstein Buchverlage GmbH, Berlin, 2010,
ISBN 978-3-7934-2193-1

Translation: Nick Handforth; www.citylanguages.de

ISBN 978-1-84850-321-2

Printed and bound in Great Britain by CPI Bookmarque, Croydon CR0 4TD.

All of the papers used in this product are recyclable, and made from wood
grown in managed, sustainable forests and manufactured at mills certified to
ISO 14001 and/or EMAS.

Contents

CONTENTS

++++

Introduction

Dear Reader,

You may have already read one of my books on wishing or cosmic ordering, but in case this is the first book on the subject you have chosen (or been given), I would like to begin by explaining briefly what 'cosmic ordering' is all about.

Cosmic ordering means asking the whole of creation for help when you have a problem you can't solve yourself.

I call it the Cosmos, but you could call it God, Creation, your guardian angel, Allah, your higher self – or whatever form of address you feel most comfortable with.

The way I see it, our universe is a whole that consists of parts – us. God didn't create the world, but rather became the world. If you look at it from this perspective, we are all individual parts of a living whole and, in essence, all is one.

If everything is one, then it doesn't matter how you choose to address this oneness or any part of it (in the sense that each form of address is equally valid). We are always seeking contact with ourselves. We are independent parts of this oneness, but we are always connected to the whole. The entire cosmos listens to us constantly, and it answers and reacts to the messages we send out.

The only question is whether we hear the answers.

I have written this little book of 21 Golden Rules and exercises to enable us to better hear and understand these answers.

THE MORE JOYFUL AND CHILDLIKE YOUR APPROACH TO LIFE IS, THE LESS THERE IS TO DO

Many Indian gurus believe that the world was not created for us to work to repay the debt for our sins. If that were true, the world would never have been created in order for there to be no opportunities for sinning. In the Far East, people are convinced that God created the world simply out of joy, and that mankind expresses God's regard for the wonder of creation, in that man has become the protector of all living things. A lack of care for other humans, animals and nature thus shows a lack of values.

The view of these masters is that happy people are closest to godliness and their own creative power, as happiness is the resonance of godliness.

The more you are thankful for and value life, the happier and more childishly unself-conscious you are, and the easier it is for you to automatically allow life to direct and lead you. Anyone who incorporates singing, dancing and childish play in their life is being led by the cosmos and can hear the answers it provides. This person probably does not need to read this book, as they will already have everything they need to communicate with the cosmos.

The more we lose our joy in existing in the present moment, or the stiffer, more blunted and joyless we have already become in our daily lives, the more practice we will need to find our way back to our true natures and to always hear the voice of the cosmic delivery man in time.

THE STATE OF OUR INNER SELF CREATES THE ENVIRONMENT AROUND US

There was recently an interesting post about this in my forum at www.baerbelmohr.de. Someone had read the book *Ich weiß, was du denkst* (*I Know What You Are Thinking* – not available in English) by Thorsten Havener and had found a description of a study by Richard Wiseman in it.

Wiseman was looking for people who described themselves either as lucky devils or jinxes. He then carried out an experiment with both groups of people, similar to the 'moonwalking bear' awareness test on YouTube (www.youtube.com/watch?v=Ahg6qcgoay4). In this test, a team in white and a team in black are playing a ball game, and you have to count how often the white team passes the ball. So you focus entirely on the white team and dutifully count the number of passes. And when, at the end, the commentator asks if you saw the dancing bear moonwalking over the court, most people can't believe it: 'Bear? What bear?' is their response.

In the video, a person dressed in a bear costume really does dance right through the players, and most viewers fail to spot him. Why? It's very simple. You didn't order a bear from the cosmos, and so your consciousness filtered it out ...

Or, to put it another way, you were concentrating so hard on counting and not making a mistake that you didn't notice the bear.

✦✦✦✦

The results from the lucky devils and the jinxes study were similar. Both groups were asked to count the number of images on a page of a newspaper. In the middle, there was a huge advertisement with the following message: *'You will win £100 if you tell your tester that you have seen this advert.'*

Almost all of the lucky devils saw the advert and won the money. But the jinxes put themselves under so much pressure to count the number of images that they always overlooked the advert.

This is a wonderful example of how our inner state creates the environment around us. When we are under stress or pressure, feel angry, have low self-esteem, etc., it is all too easy for us to overlook the opportunities that life offers, and our intuition and inner compass are turned off – drowned out by stress. We continually meet resistance instead of achieving what we desire.

People who approach things in a relaxed way, however (such as people who are convinced that they are lucky devils), have their senses open to

✦✦✦✦

new opportunities, and their intuition and inner compass work perfectly.

Therefore, our most important task every time is to make and keep ourselves receptive to cosmic deliveries, wish-fulfilment and intuitive inputs. We don't have to use our powers of persuasion to make the cosmos deliver, but rather have to learn to open our heart and eyes so that we recognise its deliveries.

FREE WILL COMES FROM INSIDE

The example in my forum was discussed in relation to the the question of free will. I also like the opinion of the Indian gurus on this point; it provides an explanation for the results of the lucky-jinx experiment:

'A person is not free to choose their actions, as these will always lead to the same results, according to their inner beliefs, convictions and character traits. A person, however, is completely free to change these inner beliefs, convictions and character traits. If they change these, their external life will automatically change.'

In other words, based on what the cosmos delivers, we can determine the state of our inner self. It never gets boring, but remains a source of constant fascination.

I hope you enjoy learning the 21 Golden Rules for Cosmic Ordering and, most importantly, I wish you every success.

Love,

Bärbel Mohr

How to Work
with this Book

I have only written half of this book – the other half is for you to write yourself. This is why it is a good idea always to have a pen handy while reading. I have suggested exercises that you can carry out for each Rule. These are lists, affirmations or thoughts that you can write down in this book below each Rule, just for yourself.

Writing something down is an epiphany in itself and has a completely different effect than if you only think about it, speak about it or imagine it. By writing, you will begin to make the Rules part of your life.

I give you the exercises as suggestions, to make the process of writing easier. But you should also write down everything else that occurs to you while reading. The best Rules are the ones you write for yourself.

The more you write in this book, the more it will become your very own cosmic order.

RULE 1

❧

The World Around You
Reflects the World
Inside You

1

~~~

Cosmic ordering requires you to realise that the world around you is a reflection of the world inside you. If I want to change the world around me, I first have to examine my inner self, and change it.

❧ EXAMPLE

If I don't love myself, the outside world reflects this in rejection by others, or at best recognition from people who don't suit me. If I do love myself, straight away I receive a great deal more friendliness and recognition from exactly the kind of people who do suit me. This is how my inner self creates what I experience in the world around me.

If you want to find out what is currently going on inside you, all you have to do is to look at what is happening in your life at the moment. How do other people treat you? What events are happening right now? For almost everything, you can ask yourself how it reflects your inner self and how you can improve a little on the inside.

 **Exercise**

When you find everyone around you irritating, you can consciously examine each of them in your mind with the following questions:

What can I learn from this person?

What reflects the beauty of this person's soul?

What is the highest potential of this person?

What best expresses the love at the core of this person?

The feeling of irritation is guaranteed to subside and a new reality will begin to unfold in your life.

What changes when you do this exercise?

How do your feelings change?

What happens? Do the other people react differently now? Do you react differently?

Keep notes below, review your notes frequently and repeat the exercise. Write down the names of the people in your environment and, next to each name, what you can learn from them, what reflects the beauty of their soul, their greatest potential and what expresses the love at the core of their being.

🌿 EXAMPLES

Peter is annoyed with his colleague Kai, who he thinks is being uncooperative. But the question *What can I learn from Kai?* makes Peter realise that he himself says 'Yes' rather too often and doesn't dare to say 'No', even occasionally. He can learn from Kai how to say 'No' and to stand up for what he thinks. But this doesn't mean he has to be as rigorous as Kai in doing so. And when Peter learns to say 'No' himself, he also finds it easier to set better boundaries for Kai – and isn't annoyed with him any more, as Kai no longer has to reflect what Peter still has to learn. The lesson has been completed.

Anna has reservations about Dagmar, and their relationship isn't exactly rosy right now either. When Anna begins to look out for the beauty in Dagmar's soul, Dagmar suddenly acts more openly and with more friendliness towards her. How come? Dagmar also notices that Anna is showing a new openness towards her, meaning she feels more comfortable with Anna, without being able to explain why.

Tip: You might not find this exercise very easy at first. If so, try it for just one person initially. You can then keep coming back to this exercise later. You will find points in many of the following Rules that will make this exercise easier.

RULE 2

~

See Only Love or the Call for Love

2

When we don't feel loved enough, this concept, taken from many spiritual teachings, can help us: fundamentally only love or fear exist. The realisation that someone who does not act lovingly does so because of a secret fear or an old, suppressed, unresolved pain is incredibly liberating. This means that no one ever treats me badly because there is something wrong with me, but rather because they have a pain, or a fear, that they have not yet resolved and therefore are incapable of acting lovingly at the moment.

Following this thought through helps to give us back our strength. We neutralise the fear and reformulate it:

Only love exists, or 'the call for love'.

Isn't this wonderful?

 Example

My colleague keeps making me look bad in front of the boss, telling him about all the things I have supposedly messed up. The normal reaction is: *He only wants to make himself look better, the stupid old creep.*

The more progressive way to look at this is: *A-ha, is he afraid of something? Maybe he feels that his job is too much for him and hopes that no one will notice that if he diverts attention from himself. Hmm, what else could it be? What could be his hidden fear?*

A question for true experts: *Where is the hidden call for love in this behaviour? Does he actually want more recognition and love from me? Does his behaviour just express general pain and a feeling of rejection? How can I give him the feeling of being welcome?*

There is probably some truth in all of this. It is just a question of how you feel most comfortable looking at the situation. Which approach gives you back the most strength and inner peace?

 **Exercise**

Make a list. In your life currently, who is calling out for love through their unloving behaviour?

Who is calling out for my love?

....

....

....

....

....

....

....

....

....

....

....

....

....

....

....

....

....

....

Can you think of any other ways you would like to respond to this kind of behaviour, if you view it as an indirect and unconscious call for love?

RULE 3

~

Expectations Create Reality
– Especially When They
Are Unconscious

3

We know from Pavlov's dogs that if we ring a bell every time we give a dog food, it will expect to be fed whenever it hears the bell ring. It will also begin to salivate, even if it isn't given anything to eat. This reaction has become an unconscious, conditioned automatic reflex.

When do you react in a similarly conditioned way in your life, without questioning the reason behind your reaction?

✻ EXAMPLE

In India, some people apparently chain young elephants to logs from which they cannot escape, no matter how hard they try. A fully grown elephant chained to the same log would easily be able to free itself, but it doesn't even try. So a fully grown elephant can be held captive using the same small log to which it became accustomed as a calf. Its experience and expectations tell it that it won't be able to escape, even though in reality just a sharp tug would be enough to free it.

Ask yourself, which parts of your life are still controlled by out-of-date expectations? Where would just a sharp tug set you free?

 **Exercise**

Whenever something hasn't worked out well, ask yourself whether you are surprised or if you 'hadn't expected anything better anyway'.

Think about what you want to achieve and create a kind of mantra or affirmation out of it that begins like this:

I allow myself …

....

I have earned the right to experience ...

....

I allow myself ...

....

I have earned the right to experience ...

....

I allow myself ...

....

I have earned the right to experience ...

....

I allow myself ...

....

I have earned the right to experience ...

....

I allow myself ...

....

I have earned the right to experience ...

....

I allow myself ...

....

I have earned the right to experience ...

....

I allow myself ...

....

I have earned the right to experience ...

....

RULE 4

~

What You Are and How You Feel Affects Others

4

⌒

When I am suffering emotional pain, certain neurons in the pain centre in my brain are activated. As soon as another person encounters me, their pain centre receives the same activation. Their so-called mirror neurons* mimic the way I am feeling. This usually takes place at a subconscious level.

This also means that the human resources manager who is looking at your application feels the same way you do. Are you full of self-

---

* *Warum ich fühle, was du fühlst* [*Why I Feel What You Feel*] is the self-explanatory title of the book by Joachim Bauer on mirror neurons (see Further Reading, page 189).

confidence or full of self-doubt? The way you feel will have a decisive effect on the decision made by the human resources manager. Once again, your inner state is shaping the world around you.

The same thing happens with potential new partners, who feel attracted or repelled according to how you are feeling (full of self-love or self-doubt). A new partner, a new boss, even a new landlord will react most positively to people with whom they feel a resonance and a positive attraction.

In all of these situations, your inner state with its expectations, your fundamental attitude to life, your fears, your trust and your conditioned reflexes all determine the outcome of the situation. We are all connected to each other and constantly exchange information on an unconscious level. Even if your conscious mind doesn't notice most of this exchange, the information still has an effect.

So the most important thing you can do to ensure that your wish is fulfilled is raise your level of self-love and self-esteem.

As we saw in the first Rule, the world around us is a reflection of the world within us, and this is particularly true for our social environment.

Other people react to how I behave and how I feel. Those who don't love themselves will receive little love from other people. This isn't unfair; this is simply life mirroring our internal state of being.

Exercise

Regularly stand naked in front of the largest mirror you have and love yourself, just the way you are. Love every part of yourself and thank your body for making it possible for you to exist on this planet. The more lovingly you treat yourself and your body, the healthier you will be as well.

Keep a self-love diary. Begin by writing down everything that went well for you as a child, a teenager, a twenty-something, a thirty-something, etc. What are you proud of? What have you done well in your life so far? Write it down.

What have you done well so far this year? Is there anything you can be proud of? Write it down! What worked out well last month, last week, yesterday and today?

This is where you can start to write a bullet-point list of all the things you have done well in your life so far:

....

....

....

....

....

....

....

....

....

....

....

....

....

....

....

....

....

....

....

....

....

....

I advise you to buy a beautiful large notebook to keep your daily diary notes in, one that you really like. Use it like a diary. Write in it every day.

Every morning, when you get up, you can have a quick look in your self-love diary and read one, two or three things that you have done well at some point in your life. And in the evening, you can write down what you have done well during the day. It is important for your self-esteem to start and end each day positively.

 The no. 1 self-love rule in daily life is:

Make a stronger committment to yourself! Take time for yourself and your needs. Look inside yourself to feel what you need, and make sure you have enough time and space to address the needs of your own body, your soul and your spirit.

Write down 10 things you are going to do for yourself:

1. ....

2. ....

3. ....

4. ....

5. ....

6. ....

7. ....

8. ....

9. ....

10. ....

RULE 5

~

Allow Yourself to Have Negative Thoughts

5

❧

Negative thoughts often aren't the real problem. They are only the starting point, from which a problem can then grow.

🌿 EXAMPLE

Let's imagine that I have just written an article that I am not completely happy with and I think: 'I haven't managed to write this article well, it's absolutely terrible.' Is it a problem to have a thought like this? No, not yet; it depends on how I develop it, whether I allow this initial thought to grow into a problem or not.

If I am being purely negative, I continue the thought with:

- *'I haven't managed to write this article well, it's absolutely terrible. I am simply too stupid; I've probably lost my inspiration and ability to write well, forever. I will never be able to write anything worthwhile ever again. I'm done for, my career is over. Oh God, what should I do? I'm as good as ruined. Everyone will turn their backs on me ...'*

But I could also think:

- *'I haven't managed to write this article well, it's absolutely terrible. Hmm, let me feel inside myself: will it be enough to do a couple of breathing exercises, to consciously centre myself, to reconnect with the source of inspiration within me? Should I take a break or wait until tomorrow to start writing again? It's not the end of the world, I usually like what I have written, and enjoy reading it. I'm sure that the next article will be a return to form.'*

Another possibility:

* *'I haven't managed to write this article well, it's absolutely terrible. I have to start all over again. But I am afraid it will turn out to be rubbish again. I know that I won't be able to write well when I keep getting myself down with all these negative thoughts. I have to think positively – that is very important right now. Oh heavens, I don't think I can do it. I'm actually the biggest fool on earth, but no one has noticed yet. I should be able to see everything in a positive light, but just how could it happen? How could I have produced such a bad article? What will everyone think?'*

And a final variant:

* *'I haven't managed to write this article well, it's absolutely terrible. How amusing, it really is a pile of mind-numbingly boring rubbish. To be honest, I had the trip tomorrow morning at the back of my mind the whole time; there was no way I could produce anything good. But I know that through lightness of being*

I will be able to write a new piece that I'm satisfied with and that will make me feel good again. And no one else is forced to like what I write. People can read what I have written if they want to and enjoy it, but no one is forced to read it. It would be awful if I had to publish things that I didn't feel happy with, or where I was always trying to guess whether everyone else would like them or not. But that isn't the case. So, everything is fine. I will always be able to write pieces in such a way that I am happy with them.'

Do you see the problem? The problem isn't the first negative thought, but the way we treat the negative thought.

Are you afraid of negative thoughts?

This will make you feel stressed.

Do you feel guilty because you have negative thoughts?

This will immediately increase your stress level.

ALLOW YOURSELF TO HAVE NEGATIVE THOUGHTS

Do you blame the thoughts and at the same time blame yourself for having them?

Oops, you are piling on even more stress!

The solution is simply to coexist with the negative thoughts and the bad feelings, and to allow yourself to have the thoughts without condemning yourself for having them. How about thinking like this: 'Oh dear, have I let myself get sucked into a spiral of negative thoughts again? Never mind, I love myself anyway. I hope everyone feels the same: let every person learn to accept and love themselves with all of their faults and weaknesses. I love even my negative thoughts. I allow them to exist.'

Every negative thought we suppress will continue to grow and prosper, until it becomes overpowering. Why? Because it craves attention. It wants to be fully felt through, then it will move on of its own accord. How come? You will find out in Rule 7.

 **Exercise**

When negative thoughts appear, allow yourself
to have them and reassure yourself that you love
yourself in spite of them, and that it is completely
normal for every person to have negative
thoughts from time to time.

Also think: 'God bless this silly thought' (or
whoever you like, the angels, the cosmos, the
source of all creation). If every negative thought
is blessed, you will automatically get rid of your
guilty conscience, because you have turned the
thought into something positive. The self-inflicted
torturous cycle will rapidly come to an end.

Remember the last negative thought that you
had. Below it write: 'And may God (the cosmos,
my guardian angel ...) bless this thought!'

....

....

....

....

....

....

....

....

....

....

....

....

....

....

....

....

....

RULE 6

~

Allow Yourself to Be Happy

6

Of course I allow myself to be happy. It is the most normal thing in the world. If you agree with me, then I am happy, because you are right. Happiness is our inherent birthright.

Many people still carry a subconscious pattern of thought inside them, however, that the purpose of life is to work off a burden of sin, and that they will end up in hell if they ever find happiness on earth. This means that they have a subconscious deadly fear of happiness. No wonder they are subconsciously constantly fighting against it.

Happiness is not only okay, it is our natural state of being ...

If you have the feeling that remnants of such thought patterns, inherited from your ancestors, might be slumbering inside you, counter them with the following exercises:

 **Exercise**

In your mind, imagine your fear of happiness, wrap it up in love and take it completely into your heart. Say to yourself:

'It is okay that I once believed that "I am not allowed to be happy". I forgive myself for everything I have laid in the way of achieving of happiness and I love myself in spite of this.'

....

....

....

....

....

Tell yourself this, and feel the words with all your heart:

'From now on, it is okay to be happy. Only when I feel enough happiness in my life will I be able to pass on some of this happiness to others. For this reason alone, it is fine to be as happy as possible.'

....

....

....

....

....

RULE 7

~

Happiness Is Your Natural State

7

⁓

Negative feelings that have been fully felt through (a pre-condition is that you are psychologically healthy; sick people will need help with this) turn into their polar opposites or evaporate completely. Why? Because being happy is our natural state of being. No baby arrives in the world feeling depressed or full of self-doubt.

The biggest impediment to happiness is thinking that we have to do so much, own so much and work so hard in order, at the end of the long journey, to be happy. The idea that being happy might be our natural state is beyond comprehension for many of us.

The tasks we give ourselves, however, differ completely depending on whether we think 'I must work hard to achieve happiness' or 'Happiness is my natural state.'

🌿 EXAMPLE

Many Sufis believe that happiness is the natural state of being for mankind. Therefore everything that makes us feel unhappy is an unnatural and artificial husk, which we ourselves have laid, layer by layer, around the true core of our being. And, just as turbulent, turbid water quickly clears when it comes to rest and the mud has a chance to settle to the bottom, our natural happiness will resurface within us when we find peace within ourselves. Silent retreats are therefore one method Sufis use to give the true core of their being space to show itself again.

Indian gurus usually choose more active methods, but they also believe that happiness is our natural state of being. For them, God is pure happiness. The happier we are, the nearer we are to the source of godliness within ourselves.

A happy person, therefore, is one who is also most in tune with their own power of creativity. A happy person places their cosmic order and, hey presto, the answer arrives.

IN THE STATE OF HAPPINESS, I BECOME ONE AGAIN WITH GODLINESS

The more unhappy we are, the further away from God we move. Being unhappy also means criticising God and saying that His/Her creation is not good enough. When we are unhappy, the godliness at our core wants to show us that we are on the the wrong path and are travelling away from our true selves. Thus it makes us sick, creates obstacles, irritations, all sorts of things. This is the way our godly core tries to remind us that we are distancing ourselves from it.

Try to imagine that the source of creation within you is lovely and warm. The further you travel away from it, the colder it gets. An occasional cool wind can be a nice adventure, but when your toes start to freeze from the cold, it is time to go back.

The Indian gurus believe that we have lost our way and can no longer find the path back to the warming source at our core, even though the way is not far. The moment I notice my freezing toes and look at them without blaming myself, and can say to myself, 'Whatever I do in my life, I will always be a wonderful, lovable being. I love myself, even in the depths of the deepest winter,' then – ta dah! – you will feel the warmth returning. As soon as you can honesttly say a sentence like this to yourself, and truly feel it in your heart of hearts, you will hardly manage to finish the word 'winter' before spring arrives.

 **Exercise**

Sit yourself down each day for at least 10 minutes. Examine your current state of being, open and honestly. Don't suppress anything, allow everything to be as it is, and be with yourself in love:

'I love and respect myself from the bottom of my heart, just the way I am.'

No matter how low you feel in your life, when you begin this exercise, the light will begin to gather within you again, if you truly feel this way.

RULE 8

~

Light Gathers Within You

8

Have you seen the water crystal photographs by Masaru Emoto? Emoto freezes droplets of water and examines their structure under the microscope. He has discovered that water reacts to every external message and influence: if you take two glasses of tap water, and stick a note on one of them with the words 'hate', 'fear', 'destruction', this water will not form any crystals, only an ugly, formless film.

If, however, you stick a note on the other glass with the words 'love' and 'thankfulness', then this water will form beautiful crystals.

The interesting thing about crystals is that they capture light. Each particle of light that falls on a crystal is caught and, as the light rebounds within the crystal, reflected back and forth, the crystal soon begins to glow with a beautiful light. When, on the other hand, light falls on a formless film, it simply passes through it and only a cheerless darkness and formlessness remains.

This type of water crystal is very ethereal, and is only visible when the droplet of water freezes under the microscope.

Every sound also causes patterns to form in ethereal structures, which in turn only become visible using certain little tricks.

Ernst F.F. Chladni (1756–1827) was the first to spread fine-grain sand on glass plates and to cause them to vibrate using the bow of his violin. The resulting patterns in the sand are called 'Chaldinian sound sculptures'.

In 1960, the Swiss doctor Hans Jenny carried out similar experiments with a vaiety of materials and even fluids (he wrote a book on this, called *Cymatics*). Alexander Lauterwasser followed in his footsteps (his book is *Water Sound Images*); among other experiments he put droplets of water on steel plates, subjected them to sound waves from loudspeakers and photographed the results.

All of these experiments demonstrate that harmonious sounds, words and even thoughts create harmonious forms in ethereal structures, which we can make visible using little tricks. Even a lovely, healthy 'A' tone has no visible form. Only through patterns in the sand do we see that a clear tone gives rise to clear forms, while a distorted wrong note creates only formless confusion.

If we apply this knowledge to our spirit and the power of our spirit, it becomes clear that, for example, every thought we have has an effect on the quality of the water in our cells and on how much light each cell does or doesn't contain.

It also becomes clear that you can feel as low as it is possible to be, but as soon as you sing a single clear note, or think a single kind thought, the most beautiful ethereal patterns and crystals form in your cellular water and in your energy fields. You immediately return to being a capturer of light and you begin to glow with ethereal brightness.

YOU DECIDE, EVERY SECOND, WHETHER TO CAUSE THE LIGHT WITHIN YOU TO GLOW, OR WHETHER TO SHOO IT AWAY AND ALLOW IT TO PASS BY

Every loving thought attracts light and strengthens you.

Every unforgiving thought dissolves the structure within you and the light escapes.

Exercise 1

Every forgiving thought is good for you, as it brings light into your being.

Into which areas of your life could you bring more light by changing your attitude?

Feel within yourself while you are doing this, and see if you can feel an increase of light within you.

Tip: Forced positive thinking ('I have to be positive, right now; my God, what a loser I am for not being able to think positively all the time') will have the opposite effect and gives rise to more self-criticism.

As soon as you can feel that a certain thought does you good, that it creates an immediate, enlightening and liberating effect inside you, it will increasingly cause a natural need within you to think more of these positive thoughts. Don't force yourself, and love yourself even if it doesn't work. Embrace your being, be with yourself, even if it feels hard to do so right now. This is precisely how you generate light: by accepting yourself unconditionally and by never blaming yourself.

Mantra: 'Even if I am the biggest fool on earth, I accept myself in love, just the way I am. I love myself, no matter what.'

How do you feel using this mantra? Make notes to create your own, personalised powerful mantra. To which areas of your life can you also bring more light by viewing yourself and others with an attitude of forgiveness?

....

....

....

....

....

....

....

....

....

Exercise 2

The Indian gurus mentioned above (with their view that happiness is our natural state of being) ask their followers to sing and dance for hours on end. They know that this causes light-capturing crystals to form at an ethereal level, which reawakens the godliness within each person. Natural feelings of happiness then resurface by themselves as soon as enough light has collected within the body.

This process takes place completely independently of all external conditions, but it has a harmonising effect on these external conditions.

YOUR REALITY UNFOLDS ITSELF BEFORE YOU IN A NEW WAY WHEN YOU RADIATE HAPPINESS AND LIGHT

Sing your favourite song out loud, and listen to yourself singing it. Try to sing it so that it sounds happy and harmonious. Also try to allow thankfulness to enter the resonance in your voice. You will be more complete and healthy on all levels and your intuition and connection to your inner light will stabilise.

Tip: Singing and dancing at the same time has an even more powerful effect.

RULE 9

~

Our Subconscious Filters

9

As soon as you or your partner gets pregnant, it seems as though pregnant women are all around you.

Or you drive along a long shopping street in an unfamiliar city looking for a flower shop. At the end of the street, somebody asks you if you saw a chemist's in the street. You probably have no idea, as you were looking out for a flower shop. Our consciousness filters out everything it deems unimportant for us at that moment.

By deciding what you want to achieve in life, or what your next step should be, you recalibrate your inner filter so that it can see and recognise new opportunities.

If you only know what you *don't* want, the filter remains calibrated for what you don't want and you continue only to notice the things you really would prefer to avoid.

'I don't want to see a flower shop', isn't a message your subconscious can understand. It will just see flower shops. You will only begin to consciously notice toy shops when you begin to be interested in toy shops and set your filter for them.

 **Exercise**

Many people find it difficult to decide what they want. They only know what they don't want (but even then there is help – see Rule 17).

Write down below what you still want to achieve in life (I recommend using a soft pencil). Review these notes regularly, correct or rub out your list and keep working on it until you have something that no longer changes or hardly changes. When you are clear about what you want, then the cosmos can create clear opportunities for you to achieve it.

....

....

....

....

....

....

....

....

....

....

....

....

RULE 10

~⌇~

The Shortest Path Is Not the Only Route to Your Goal

10

~~~

We understand reaching a goal in a direct linear way as using our logical mind to determine where we currently find ourselves, where we want to get to, and what the best and most logical way to reach our goal would be. For example: I am at point A at the moment, I want to reach point B, so off I march directly towards it. It is often not as easy as that in real life, however.

But luckily there is also the non-linear way to reach your goals. No matter where you are, you decide where you want to get to, you let the cosmos know and allow yourself to be led to your goal by the cosmos.

How can this possibly work?

🌿 Example

The Russian Academy of Sciences has been carrying out research for 40 years that proves that every proton and electron in the universe (i.e. all sub-atomic particles) knows precisely, to within one metre, where it is in the universe at any moment. Each particle is also able to swap information with all the other particles in the universe at any time. Whenever a proton wants to go somewhere, it can find out the information it requires from the entire universe. It knows where it is and how to get to the new location it wishes to reach.

How does this help us? Your entire body, like every other object in the universe, consists of atoms. These in turn are made up of protons and electrons. This means that your entire body is a natural navigation system, and every single tiny particle inside you knows at any point in time where you are in the world and where you need to go in order to reach your chosen goal.

So you don't need anything else, just yourself.

✦✦✦✦

And yet most of us seem to be stuck in places we don't want to be for long periods every day. We spend too little time in communication with ourselves, with the knowledge hidden within us and with our inner voice.

Maybe you could tell your conscious mind a bit more often that everything in the cosmos is connected and is constantly swapping information.

We can all allow the voice within us to steer us to places that we wouldn't be able to find using our logical mind.

To achieve this, we have to practise communicating with our inner voice and nurture the acute perception of our own feelings and intuition. Only a great deal of practice will allow us increasingly to separate intuition from pre-conceived ideas, and to hear the directions being sent out by our sub-atomic navigation system.

This is actually happening. There are already industrial applications being developed that will render the old satellite navigation systems obsolete and replace them with more simple, sub-atomic navigation systems. This is already technically possible. But the most accurate navigation system is you yourself, once you are fully back in contact with yourself.

 **Exercise**

Go outside, sit down in natural surroundings, and just listen to nature: how it rustles, scratches, murmurs, hums, trills and chirps. Just imagine that you could speak with nature. Just imagine that no noise is coincidental. Imagine that there is knowledge and truth hidden within all the chirping and rustling. What is it trying to say to you?

Then close your eyes and listen within yourself (you can also do this at home). Listen to your breathing. What are you trying to tell you about yourself?

Lay your hand on your heart and listen to its beat.
What is it trying to say?

In your mind, stroke your body from inside with
spiritual hands. Send love and thankfulness into
every part of your body.

The better connected you are to yourself and your
innermost nature, the more clearly you will hear,
notice and react completely subconsciously to
your inner compass. Everything you need is there
already. You need absolutely nothing else. You
need only be more closely in tune with yourself
in order to retrieve and use all of the information
that is already there. All the knowledge in the
world is within you, just as it is all around you. It is
easier to search for it within yourself than to look
for it outside.

But you can still include your conscious mind in
this process; it is equally important, otherwise we
wouldn't have one. To live fully means unifying
heart with mind, and not ignoring either of them.

Exercise

What do you hear? What messages and ideas arise within you when you listen closely to yourself and to nature? Write them down:

....

....

....

....

....

....

....

....

....

....

....

RULE 11

Most of the Things You
Create Serve Your Best
Interests on a Spiritual
Level; Trust in Yourself

11

⌒

'What? I'm supposed to trust myself? Even though the stupid cosmos still hasn't delivered my millions? If only I had that money, everything would be okay ...'

This is what a lot of people think, yet there is hardly a more frustrated group in society than millionaires whose millions have already been delivered. We often wish for things that, if they were delivered, would make us feel worse rather than better.

✣ EXAMPLE

Here is an example to illustrate this. You will surely be able to think of similar experiences of your own. Nine-year-old Johanna tells her mother that she would like to be a child photo model and asks her mother to find out how she can do this.

'You know I am under a lot of time pressure at the moment, my love. You'll have to order it from the cosmos. I can't support your wish at the moment, I'm sorry,' is the answer.

'All right then, I'll order it from the cosmos,' thinks the child to herself, and immediately does so. A short while later she is at a friend's house playing. Her friend's parents are being visited by a photographer, who also takes photos of children. She looks at Johanna and says to her, 'You have quite a good look. Would you like to come to a casting photoshoot with me?'

Johanna certainly does. She appears at the next possible casting and does so well that she is booked immediately for a job. A photoshoot is also about whether you can act in a natural way in front of the camera, with character and self-confidence. Johanna can manage this and is promptly booked for a job for a magazine for parents. Her mother is amazed at how quickly her little daughter made her wishes come true.

However, I met mother and daughter a short time after and I asked Johanna how the photoshoot had gone. 'Boring,' she answered. 'You aren't allowed to do anything yourself, you have to do exactly what they say. And you spend most of the time sitting around waiting.' She had crossed the aim of being a child photo model off her wish list. It had been her greatest dream, but shortly after it had come true she realised that this dream was no fun in real life.

This is often the case: we dream feverishly of how wonderful it would be 'If only...', not realising how little fun it would be if it really came true.

Begin by trusting your inner wisdom more and believing that it always wants the best thing possible for you. You can do this by being thankful for the little happy moments you have each day. By doing this, you will support and help your soul to find its way to fulfilling its greatest potential, all by itself.

Being thankful and making the most of each moment is like turning your inner navigation system to the 'autopilot for happiness' setting. Because if all you do is whinge about the way your life is at present, you are criticising the godliness within you. This is like giving yourself a vote of no-confidence. Thank yourself for your life and trust in yourself. Your inner wisdom will reward you richly for it.

 **Exercise**

Each day, write down something that you are thankful for:

- *I am thankful for my bed*

- *I am thankful for my clothes.*

- *I am thankful for the food I eat,*

    ... for my life,

    ... my friends,

... my family,

... the book in my hands,

... the carpet,

... the lightbulb,

... the plug ...

Yup – you can even be thankful for the
plug. I learned that from my children. They
spontaneously created a song of thanks about a
year ago. It contained a list of about 200 things
for which they were thankful (including the plug,
air, socks, flies on the wall, etc.). And the chorus
was: 'Aaand – I love everything! Ev-ery-thing,
everything!'

I am thankful for my children. Most of what I
learn I learn from them, or through them.

What are you thankful for?

....

....

....

....

....

....

....

....

....

....

....

....

....

....

....

RULE 12

~∽~

Our Problems Are Trying to Help Us

12

What is it that makes so many millionaires feel unhappy, even though they appear to have everything? *That* is precisely the problem – having everything!

The Chinese have a curse: 'May all your wishes be fulfilled!' What lies behind this is a deep understanding of the human psyche. When we no longer have any dreams and nothing to strive for, aimlessness and frustration set in. On the other hand, having an obstacle to overcome, being able to achieve something, to experience yourself as someone who can make things happen brings real satisfaction.

🌿 Example

When I was 24, I lived in an apartment with no hot water, actually without any running water at all (there was just a cold-water tap in the hall outside the apartment). There was also only a stinky coke stove in the kitchen, and otherwise no other heating at all. Shower, hand basin, sink, heating – all were non-existent. And I won't even begin to tell you about the wonderful neighbours. Some of you might remember the example from my very first book about the neighbour who would shout loudly across the courtyard at night, and who I was only able to get to be quiet with great difficulty.

But I don't think I mentioned the lady who lived in the apartment below me, who had 20 cats and no kitty toilet, and so had rotting cat poo all over her floor. And also not that at some point the cat fleas began to crawl up her walls and into our apartment.

I also left out that some of my post regularly went missing.

I had an interesting conversation recently with a young woman, 22 years old. She is, in all honesty, disatisfied with her three-room apartment in a modern block. This and that isn't good, the apartment is too expensive, she never has any money, and so on and so forth. I showed her photos of my flat, described above. She was appalled. After we had chatted for a while, we had the idea of feeling our way into the two situations. I imagined that I was 24 and living in her apartment, and she that she was living in my former apartment.

The weird thing was, in my mind, I was far more disatisfied living in her apartment than I had ever been in mine, while she felt happy imagining that she was living in my old apartment.

'There would be so many things I could improve in such a wreck of a place that I would also have the courage to do. I am sure I would find someone who would put in a bathroom and kitchen for me. It would be a great adventure ...,' she mused.

And that is exactly what happened back then. A friend came to live with me for six months and fitted everything: hot water, a kitchen, bathroom and heating. The place still looked quite rustic, more like a tree house than a normal flat, but that was exactly what was so great about it. In winter, we sat on cushions in the hall in front of the gas heater, which heated the entire apartment, and it felt really cosy.

There were also nice neighbours. One of them kept losing his key and always climbed through my window to get back into his apartment.

And I only had to pay 149 euros a month with all costs included (300 Deutschmarks, of course, back then). As a freelancer, I hardly had to work at all to earn that much. When I started to earn more money as a graphic designer, I kept going on trips around the world and was hardly ever at home.

When I told the young lady from the modern apartment block about this, she became very thoughtful. 'I think that is the problem. I have created a situation for myself where I feel that there is no going forward or back. I am stuck. In an apartment like yours, I would have been able to do so many things, right away. There were more problems in your apartment than in mine, but these would have been problems that I could do something about. I think I don't feel happy, because I have created obstacles for myself that are just too big. A-ha!'

The next thing she did was move out of her modern flat into a scruffy, old shared apartment. Once there, she immediately started her DIY and began to feel much better. And, shortly afterwards, she found a new line of work. The feeling of having something to do and being able to overcome her obstacles had given her more inner freedom and more self-confidence and, all of a sudden, her job applications were being answered, which until then had been unsuccessful.

This isn't to say of course that everyone would be happy moving into a scruffy, old apartment. The example shows that you have to find the place that suits you individually, which gives you the room you need to manoeuvre and develop. This can be completely different for each person. But you won't discover it if you only orient yourself towards what others are doing or what they expect of you.

Problems are opportunities. They are there to help us. The following Rules give you further suggestions on how to use problems to strengthen yourself.

 **Exercise**

Write down what you consider to be your biggest problem at the moment.

Come back to look at this page in one week, one month and in one year.

What happened to your problem? Is it still so important? Did you find a solution?

....

....

....

....

....

Underneath the problem, write down what you
most wish for at the moment.

....

....

....

....

....

....

....

....

....

....

RULE 13

~⌒~

Even Intuitive Skills
Need Practice

13

~~~

What happens to a person who applies for a job for which they aren't qualified? Either they won't get the job, or if they do they will lose it shortly afterwards when it becomes clear that they aren't up to it. If the person wants to have a job like that again, they first have to get the necessary qualifications. I can't become a tailor without first learning how to sew.

This applies not only to jobs but to the rest of our lives as well:

- *I can't have a happy relationship without gaining the social skills that allow me to have one.*

- *I can't stay healthy unless I have a clue of how to keep my body healthy: bad food, no exercise, lots of stress, being surrounded by poisons or a high level of electro-smog every day – people who live like this are unable to look after their own health.*

- *I can't become rich, or stay rich, if I am bad at dealing with money. If I spend 20 euros for every 10 I have, sooner or later I am going to have a problem.*

And the same applies to spiritual abilities:

- *A person who never looks within themselves can't expect to hear their inner voice when it has something to say.*

- *A person who never relaxes, switches off, meditates or uses another method of calming their soul will also find it difficult to make their way through our hectic world using their intuitive abilities.*

- *A person who suppresses their feelings won't be able to see the path these feelings show them.*

- *A person who never feels their way into their heart won't hear the messages their heart is sending them.*

- *The intuition of people who are subject to constant stress and tension won't work at all, as modern neuroscience has repeatedly demonstrated.*

 **Exercise**

Make a list. What do you regularly do for your body, spirit, soul and intuitive abilities?

A muscle that is never used becomes weak and wastes away. The same applies to your connection to the cosmic spirit as to your body, spirit and soul. They all waste away if we don't take care of them. It doesn't have to be much. Ten minutes of little exercises a day, directing your attention to them has a greater effect than making a large effort very sporadically.

Make notes on what little things you can regularly do for yourself:

....

....

....

....

....

....

....

....

....

....

....

RULE 14

~~~

Dealing with Obstacles Positively Makes You Strong

14

⌒

Just imagine: it's 2 a.m. and you are driving on the motorway when suddenly one of your tyres bursts, and you find that your mobile's battery is dead.

Scenario 1: You drive on to the hard shoulder, get angry, start shouting and pulling your hair out, then you start to sob and sink into a well of self-pity and depressing thoughts. Overcome by these feelings, you slump down behind the wheel.

Scenario 2: You drive on to the hard shoulder, breathe thoughts of light and love in through your nose, and blow out all shock and stress through your mouth as you breathe out. You place your hand on your belly, just below your belly button, and only breathe in as far as your hand permits until you feel calm and relaxed again. Then you get out, put on your reflective jacket and look to see which direction the nearest emergency telephone is in.

In both cases you will eventually make it home. But which will cost you more energy and tire you out more – *scenario 1* or *2*?

If you react as in *scenario 2*, you gain the knowledge that you can stay calm in a crisis, can think clearly and that this makes you feel surprisingly good; you are collecting units of energy for later life. Your self-image becomes stronger and more positive. You trust yourself more. The energy of your aura rises and your power of attraction for others and for life itself increases. And, without doing anything else, you attract more positive opportunities.

If, on the other hand, you react as in *scenario 1*, then you lose units of energy. You will emerge weaker from the situation and fear any coming problems.

Every little problem that you address constructively strengthens you for the next big obstacle. You are, so to say, collecting units of energy.

🌿 EXAMPLE

The weakest people are those who have always had someone else to sort things out for them, as they don't trust themselves with anything and feel dependent and powerless. I remember one young man who reacted with utter panic when his parents asked him to move out of the family home. He was going to a friend of mine for therapy and it turned out that he was afraid that he would not be able to get the electricity and water bills transferred into his own name or do his own washing in his new flat. These were the three points he was panicking most about. Once he had managed to do them, he came beaming to my friend and said that he didn't know how he could ever have been so stupid as to live at home for so long and hide behind his mother's apron, as freedom was so wonderful. What luck that his parents had thrown him out.

He didn't trust himself to manage anything, because he had never solved any problems himself.

Solving problems makes you strong – and even makes you feel joyful. So throw yourself into the next problem with joy. You will come out of it with greater strength than you had before.

This is also important in cosmic ordering. If you have a 100-point list in your order for your perfect partner, then it might be that they live 500 miles away. If the mere thought of telephoning the local council makes you feel afraid, how are you going to manage moving to a town 500 miles away? You will miss your delivery. A clear case of refusal to receive a delivery because of a lack of energy units.

Every problem you overcome makes you stronger and prepares you for larger deliveries of happiness from life, which are often bound to a string of changes in your life.

Exercise

Make a list. Which problems have you dealt with constructively in life so far? How did you feel afterwards?

....

....

....

....

....

....

....

....

....

....

RULE 15

～

Discover the Ancient Native American Feeling Prayer

15

⁓

The ancient Native Americans had their own particular method of cosmic ordering: they imagined what it would be like if their wish had already come true and made the image as real as possible; they felt what it would be like, precisely and carefully. When they had identified the feeling clearly, they gave thanks for it and were certain that this would pull the thing they were wishing for into their lives. They called this process the *feeling prayer* and believed it to be far more effective than a request prayer, in which the person praying has the experience of being small and weak, dependent on waiting for the grace of a higher power.

The grace, however, comes from the fact that we already contain everything, and that we only have to rediscover these powers within ourselves.

There have been countless research studies into the placebo effect over the years and some doctors are convinced that what really makes us ill, or makes an illness fatal, are fear and irreconcilability. A person who is free from fear can heal themselves of nearly anything, even in the final stages of an illness.

✤ Example

You can, for example, give two groups of people a fermented drink and tell the first group that it contains a high level of alcohol. The second group is given the same alcoholic drink, but they are told that it is just a fermented drink and contains no alcohol whatsoever. If you make sure that the person serving the drinks does not know about the test (because they might unconsciously give a clue to some of the subjects), then the members of the first group will become drunker than the second.

Experiments like this demonstrate the strength of our power of imagination and how much it influences us. The Native American feeling prayer makes positive use of this fact.

 **Exercise**

Write down your own feeling prayer. Write down how you feel when your wish has already come true. So, for example, if you are wishing for a new flat, write down how you feel in this new flat. If your wish is for a new partner, write down how you feel being with him/her.

....

....

....

....

....

....

RULE 16

～◠～

Your Mind Is the Captain, Your Emotions Are the Fuel and Motor

16

Our rational mind decides where the journey will take us, but our emotions are both the fuel and the motor.

When I am filled with worries and self-doubt, I travel at a snail's pace, but the greater my conviction and general happiness with life, the faster I reach my goals.

This means that coming to terms with our feelings is particularly important (I have written about this in my previous books).

The most important exercise for practising this is very similar to the feeling prayer. It examines the 'wish behind the wish':

Close your eyes for a moment and imagine that your greatest wish has already been fulfilled. How would you feel? And how would this feeling express itself in your body?

The wish behind the wish is always the feeling that we are actually trying to achieve, and this is different for every one of us.

🌿 EXAMPLE

One person wishes that they were completely liberated and independent in their ideal job. Another yearns for friendship and a sense of belonging within a strong team. And for yet another it's about gaining recognition.

Discover the wish feeling behind your order and order exactly that from the cosmos at the same time!

Bring this feeling to mind as often as you can, then your subconscious will recognise fitting opportunities more quickly, because they will feel like your wish feeling. This is how you fill up on fuel for the motor in your subconscious.

You will even be able to recognise your ideal partner in this way, because they will feel like the ideal partner in your internal vision. And then you will stop choosing partners according to old family patterns, but instead according to your actual wish feeling.

 **Exercise**

For everything you want to order from the cosmos, ask yourself what the wish behind the wish is.

How would you feel if you already had it? Put an order in for this feeling too and nurture it and strengthen it wherever you can in your life as well.

My wish feelings are:

....

....

....

....

....

....

....

....

....

....

....

....

....

....

....

....

....

RULE 17

~

What Should I Do If I Only Know What I Don't Want?

17

It doesn't matter at all if I only know what I don't want, because I can change this by examining my own resonance and healing it. As a result of this, a new reality automatically begins to unfold, because my changed, healed resonance begins to pull other things into my life.

Resonance, in this instance, means the power of attraction. What is it in me that attracts unloving situations or people? Perhaps, because of my fear, I keep a constant look out for them, or I reject something so categorically that I give the whole subject a great deal of energy, and therefore attract it.

🌿 EXAMPLE

Ute is an international journalist. She was under a lot of stress for a time, rushing from one appointment to the next. She finally had almost 500 finished articles on her computer and she wanted to sell these piece by piece in another country and spend some time relaxing there as well. Suddenly, her laptop caught a virus and had a total meltdown. All 500 of her articles were gone. She was appalled and completely devastated. She had somehow never thought to make a backup. Now she had lost many years of work. Ute rushed from one specialist to the other, but no one was able to extract the data from her laptop.

Ute finally decided to look inside herself, asking the question, 'What in me resonates with this, causing such a thing to happen to me?'

If you ask yourself this question while in a relaxed state, you will always discover an answer. If you ask yourself the question on several consecutive days, you might find more than one answer. They are all are part of a larger puzzle, which you used to create this situation for yourself.

Ute found out, among other things, that she was still feeling under so much pressure that she was doing herself harm. She saw the collapse of her computer as a warning signal, and heeded it to prevent her own body from collapsing.

Whatever answer you discover, then say to yourself:

- *I am sorry, I love myself in spite of this.*

- *I forgive this resonance in me and I love myself in spite of it.*

- *It is okay the way things are; I love myself the way I am.*

Choose whichever affirmation suits you best at the time, and pay attention to the emotions you feel when you say these sentences to yourself.

Either you can achieve more inner peace with this type of internal exercise, or completely new solutions will appear or become visible in your life shortly afterwards.

In Ute's case, she suddenly got to know a particularly effective hacker who, with a click of his mouse, made her 500 articles all reappear as if by magic on her hard drive, then copied them over on to her new computer.

A similar thing happened to Barbara, who felt she was being bullied by a colleague. Her colleague was young and smart, while Barbara was close to retirement and therefore wasn't so quick on her feet.

Some days, Barbara was really short of breath and felt she wasn't dealing with the situation very well.

The following question helped her:

'If I were this colleague and was behaving like her, why would I be doing this?'

and

'What is the resonance within me that makes me have a colleague like this?'

She was able to resolve the answer that she discovered with the words, 'I am sorry, I love myself in spite of it,' and the other two affirmations.

Barbara repeated this exercise whenever she had a problem with the behaviour of her younger colleague. Two weeks later, the younger colleague had a problem and only Barbara recognised this, because she had come to see through some of her colleague's idiosyncracies, as a result of her exercises. She helped her colleague discreetly, without saying a word. The younger woman was so relieved that she has acted like a completely different person ever since, and has been the very embodiment of friendliness.

She even apologised for her former behaviour and explained that she had thought that her older colleague would reject all of the innovations she was bringing to the company, just because she was new. But she saw now that she was completely mistaken. She was very sorry.

Then it was Barbara's turn to apologise. By trying to find what she had within her that was in resonance with the problem, she had discovered precisely that she was opposed to all change. But once she had forgiven herself for it, she began to enjoy the changes.

With this kind of exercise, you never have to know what you want, but only what irritates and annoys you, and what you want to change for the better.

You can find more information on this and more free exercises on my website, **www.cosmic-ordering.de**.

RULE 18

~

Use the Law of Attraction

18

〜

Does the following sound familiar? You break up with your partner and find someone new. But after just a few months your new partner starts behaving in the same awful way as your last one. Or you change jobs because you find it impossible to work there any more. Initially the new company seems to be a lot better, but after a short time everything starts going the same way as in the last job. How can this be?

This is the law of attraction, which is merciless in revealing what our deepest subconscious looks like. We can only escape this type of repetitive loop by changing the problem inside ourselves.

🌿 EXAMPLE

Indian gurus see it like this: mankind has no free will in his actions, since every action always leads to the same results if we don't alter our internal patterns. One hundred per cent of a person's free will consists of their internal patterns of belief, expectations, attitudes and inner qualities. When we change these, our next external action will automatically lead to completely new results.

From the Indian point of view, you don't need to know who, when, where or why anybody did anything to us. It is enough to continually seek to enhance and refine your own qualities and character traits.

In the same way, all our low-flying patterns from childhood, old wounds and pains automatically fall away from us when our increased resonance raises us to a level of consciousness where our new qualities either overwrite the old ones or the old ones simply fall away.

Exercise 1

Try to imagine the following: all of the old, low-vibrating patterns in your consciousness and your body are sinking down and pass through the soles of your feet into the Earth and keep sinking deep down into the Earth's core. Mother Earth transforms them there with lightness and love so that finally they reappear somewhere in the world as a brightly coloured butterfly that flutters joyfully away.

While doing this, breathe in through your nose and out through your mouth and imagine that everything you don't want is passing into the Earth.

Then hold the palms of your hands up towards the sky and imagine that you are absorbing new strength, love, thankfulness, wisdom and intuition. Pull these into your body through your palms with each breath.

With everything you encounter, listen inside yourself and ask yourself which tools would give you particular joy and strength to use when working to enhance your inner being.

Exercise 2

Thank your ancestors for giving you life and recognise the difficulties they had to overcome in their lives.

Thank all of them for putting themselves through these difficulties and so making your life possible. At the same time, return all of things to them that you might have inherited from them but no longer want to have in your life. By thanking them and giving them recognition, they will gladly take these things back and they will dissolve in the love you share.

In your mind, absorb all the positive potential from all of your ancestors and strengthen yourself through it. Also give thanks to each one of them in your thoughts for this gift.

RULE 19

~

Live in Unity

19

Living in unity with all things does not mean giving up any part of yourself.

We are all independent components of a greater whole and serve the whole precisely through our independence.

Just imagine the cells in your nose had come under the spell of a somewhat silly guru and now believed they would have to give up their independence, relinquish all individuality and subsume themselves in the unity of the muscles under the skin. Bing-bang-boom, you suddenly wouldn't have a nose any more, just smooth flat skin in its place. That would look silly, wouldn't it?

Unity has a different meaning. We are each an individual 'cell' within a larger body (for example the body of mankind) and we serve this whole best if we fully live out our individuality and the plan for our souls. Nature is clever. She ensures that each person is happiest when they are doing exactly what fits in with their soul's task. The cells in your nose are happiest when forming your nose and not when meditating on what it might be like to be a cell in your big toe.

One problem in our society is that we have belly-button cells (e.g. natural-born midwives) acting as, perhaps, lawyers, just because that was what daddy wanted. And natural head cells (e.g. lawyers) may have to become apprentice carpenters because their single-parent family didn't have enough money to send them to university. In the general frustration this causes, they all want 'at least' to earn as much money as possible, as a kind of compensation for their twisted lives.

In my view, the most important thing to achieve first is unity within yourself. Unity of body, mind and soul.

Is there a part you are neglecting? If your soul or body receives too little nourishment from you, then 'practising unity' might also mean NOT calling back a few people who want to talk to you, but instead taking some time out to rebalance yourself.

 **Exercise**

What else can I do to find and foster more unity within myself? (You will find tips for more in-depth further reading on page 191.)

Write down which part of your body, mind and soul you might be neglecting and below that what you are going to do for each part.

....

....

....

....

....

....

....

....

....

....

....

....

....

....

....

....

....

....

RULE 20

~

Allow Yourself to
Be Thankful

20

❧

Being thankful for the little things in life (as well as for the big things, of course) means opening your heart to life. And the more open your heart is, the stronger the connection will be to cosmic wisdom and the compass within you.

Whenever I close my heart, I cut myself off from the stream of energy. This isn't a very clever thing to do, but it happens to me from time to time. Then I have to remind myself to open it. Instead of getting annoyed with the person opposite me, I can ask myself:

'What can I learn from this person? What is the beauty within their soul? How does the love within this person express itself?'

✦✦✦✦

If I think, 'How can this person do ...? They should be doing ..., and why don't they do this or that? It's clear that they have to ...', I am being ungrateful to life because I am criticising the being of another person.

By making an effort to see the beauty within them, I raise my appreciation for the other person. And my reward is that the energy within me begins to flow again and I reconnect to my inner compass.

I have to admit, this often requires a huge U-turn. On the one hand, standing up for my beliefs and not letting myself be duped, and on the other, answering the call for love within the other person. But the more I practise, the more nuanced the possibilities for action become. I realise that a solution almost always exists from which both sides can profit. If I only want it. And if I don't want it, I consciously decide against it, without blaming myself at all. I am allowed to be.

But I also recognise that hurting another person is sometimes unavoidable. However, if I do this in a loving and careful way, with the intention of doing the right and just thing, the overall result and the answer from life will be very different compared to if I simply lash out with the attitude inside me of 'I am right and you are stupid.'

You can only either be right or have friends – you can't have both, according to Marshall Rosenberg, the inventor of non-violent communication. And having friends is surely much more fulfilling than being lonely and right. This is also about thankfulness. In the end, I am thankful for the friendship of others and, by valuing this, I can also occasionally do without being right.

 **Exercise**

Which areas of my life tend more to be about standing up for my beliefs rather than bending to those of others?

And which areas are more about showing thankfulness for things as they are?

Might it even be possible to unify these two, as paradoxical as it might sound at first?

This is where I could stand up for myself more:

....

....

....

....

....

This is where I could show more thankfulness:

....

....

....

....

....

Now try the exercise in Rule 1 again (see page 4).

RULE 21

~

Cosmic Ordering and Healing

21

⌒

Cosmic ordering only works long term if you have an open heart and a good 'connection to up above', which both enable you to pay attention to your inner compass and the small impulses you receive from inside.

Healing works in precisely the same way. There is no general course of therapy that works for everyone; healing always takes a very individual path. It requires an open heart and for the person in question to learn to pay close attention to the small impulses from their soul, and to trust and follow their inner compass.

The questions that help me in both areas – ordering and self-healing – are the same:

- *What is my next step on the way to healing or on the path to fulfilling my wish?*

- *How am I blocking the flow of energy?*

- *How can I open my heart more?*

- *How did I cause myself to be this situation?*

- *What is it trying to tell me?*

- *How can I come to terms with the circumstances of my unfulfilled wish, or with my illness?*

 **Exercise 1**

Make notes on the questions above.

....

....

....

....

Exercise 2

Exercise to strengthen health:

Each morning, consciously follow your breath as it flows through your body, and at the same time think about the oxygen flowing into each and every cell. Whenever you have the feeling that your breath can't pass through a certain part of your body and flow freely and unimpeded, breathe particularly deeply into this area until the feeling of free flow returns to this part.

This exercise strengthens both our ethereal awareness of ourself and automatically means that it is easier for us to hear our inner voice when it is trying to send us a message.

Summary of the 21 Golden Rules

Don't just put these Rules to one side. They are intentionally written in such a short and handy format to allow you to carry them around with you always and have a quick look inside. We actually already know all of the most important information. Now is the time to put these things into practice and to start developing your own individual style.

Working on yourself will only become really successful when it is no longer work but a process full of joy and fun in discovering and developing yourself further. Remember what the Indian gurus say about free will. What did they say again? That's right, you'd better take another quick look ...

I wish you every success and send you love on your journey of discovery and in living out your full potential.

Love,

Bärbel

Rule 1: The world around you reflects the world inside

Cosmic ordering means that you have to realise that the world around you is a reflection of the world inside you. This means you are actually making orders all the time, because everything that you encounter mirrors how you are inside.

Rule 2: Only see love or the call for love

View every unloving behaviour as a call for love. With this attitude, anger and the feeling of being under attack can dissolve into compassion and inner peace.

Rule 3: Expectations create reality – especially when they are unconscious

In which areas of your life do you have fixed expectations? Might it be worth questioning some of these? For example, if you think, 'I never could do this or that,' when was the last time you tried? Every weakness can be transformed into a strength. Give yourself a chance.

Rule 4: What you are and how you feel affects others

You radiate your fundamental attitude to life and your level of self-love out into the world around you. If you reject yourself, it is also hard for others to love you, often without them being able to say why. The way you feel about yourself transmits itself to them.

The best thing that you can do for yourself, therefore, is always to increase your level of self-love.

Rule 5: Allow yourself to have negative thoughts

Wrong: 'I am so stupid, I always think so negatively, I will never understand ...' Such thoughts or feelings of guilt will keep pulling you further down.

Right: When negative thoughts surface, allow yourself to have them and reassure yourself that you love yourself in spite of them, and that it

is completely normal for every person to have negative thoughts from time to time.

'May God/Heaven/my guardian angel/the cosmos bless these silly thoughts' is a helpful thought that you can send out after each negative thought, whenever you notice yourself having one.

Rule 6: Allow yourself to be happy

The happier you are, the more happiness you carry out into the world with you. There is no reason to feel guilty if life is treating you better than others. On the contrary, if you feel guilty, you would only contribute to increasing unhappiness. Be contagiously happy instead – then you will also be helping others.

Rule 7: Happiness is your natural state

In the state of happiness, you become one again with godliness. Being happy means you have the same resonance as the power of creation and the godly core of your being. No baby is born unhappy. Rediscover your natural joy in being.

Rule 8: Light gathers within you

You decide, each second, whether you cause the light within you to glow, or whether you scare it away and allow it to pass by. Each loving thought attracts light and increases the light within you. Every unforgiving thought dissolves the structure within you and causes the light to escape.

Rule 9: Our subconscious filters

No sooner are you or your partner pregnant than it seems as if you are surrounded by pregnant women. Our subconscious filters our perception. As soon as you formulate a clear order and send it off, it begins to filter again and to steer your attention towards the opportunities that will bring you closer to your goal.

Rule 10: The shortest path is not the only route to your goal

You have an inherent wisdom within you that can see the whole picture. Learn to listen deeply within yourself and to follow the voice of your inner compass more and more. This will help you arrive at your goal more quickly, even if your rational mind often can't then explain how you got there.

Rule 11: Most of the things you create serve your best interests on a spiritual level; trust in yourself

Being thankful and making the most of each moment is like turning your inner navigation system to the 'autopilot for happiness' setting. Because if all you do is whinge about the way your life is at present, you are criticising the godliness within you. This is like giving yourself a vote of no-confidence. Thank yourself for your life, and trust in yourself. Your inner wisdom will reward you richly for it.

Rule 12: Our problems are trying to help us

Overcoming problems and obstacles in a positive way makes us happy. A complete lack of problems and hurdles, on the other hand, leads to sloth, boredom, a lack of self-trust and unhappiness. The Chinese even have this curse: 'May all your wishes be fulfilled.'

Rule 13: Even intuitive skills need practice

What do you regularly do for your body, spirit, soul and intuitive abilities? If you never use a muscle, it will weaken and waste away. So train the 'muscles' of your intuition, so that it is always ready to be used when you need it.

Rule 14: Dealing with obstacles positively makes you strong

Love your problems and use them to help you grow. Every obstacle that you overcome increases your strength and trust in yourself, so that you can achieve ever more in life.

Rule 15: Discover the ancient Native American feeling prayer

The ancient Native Americans tried to imagine what it would be like if their wish had already come true, making the image as real as possible, and they precisely and carefully felt what it would be like. When they had identified the feeling clearly, they gave thanks for it and were certain that this would pull the thing for which they were wishing into their lives.

Rule 16: Your mind is the captain, your emotions are the fuel and motor

Your rational mind makes the decisions about where the journey is going, but emotions are both the fuel and the motor. If you are filled with worries and self-doubt, you will travel at a snail's pace, but the greater your conviction and general joy in life are, the faster you will reach your goals.

How would you like to feel, and how would you feel if the thing you're wishing for had already arrived? Strengthen this feeling in your life.

Rule 17: What should I do if I only know what I don't want?

Heal the resonance within yourself that has created the thing you don't want. Ask yourself what within you is in resonance with the person or situation you don't like. Wrap everything you find up in your love and keep loving yourself and everything you discover within yourself just the way you are.

Rule 18: Use the law of attraction

Our free will to act is only superficial, as whatever action we take causes similar results due to our internal patterns and attitudes. We have, however, 100 per cent free will in changing our inner attitudes and qualities. If we change these, we will automatically pull different results into our lives.

Rule 19: Live in unity

We are all integral parts of a larger whole. You could also say that we are all individual cells within a larger body (for example, the body of mankind) and we serve this whole best if we live out our individuality and the plan for our soul to the full.

Rule 20: Allow yourself to be thankful

Whenever you close your heart, you cut yourself off from the stream of energy. Thankfulness reopens your connection to the stream of energy.

Rule 21: Cosmic ordering and healing

Cosmic ordering only works long-term if you keep an open heart and a good 'connection to up above', which both enable you to pay attention to your inner compass and notice the small impulses your receive from inside. And healing works in exactly the same way. Both are individual processes, the key to which you will only be able to find within your own heart.

Summary of the Basic Rules for Cosmic Ordering

A summary of techniques from this and my other books on cosmic ordering.

THE BASIC RULES FOR COSMIC ORDERING

1: Make your order (as a thought or in writing, with or without lighting a candle) in a way that feels good and powerful for you personally

It doesn't matter how or where you make your order. The cosmos is always listening – it can't help it. Everything you send out, feel, believe and expect automatically creates a resonance in the cosmos and there will always be feedback.

✦✦✦✦

The difference between an order and a passing thought is clear intention and focus.

At the beginning, therefore, it can help if you write down your order and keep it in a special place. Some people like to keep a flower, a candle or a pretty stone with it. There is no right or wrong way. The only criterion is that it has to feel good to you.

There are also people who burn their orders after writing them down. Others throw them into a river, or only make orders at night, by moonlight, in the garden ... You are doing everything right if you feel good, strong and connected to the cosmos when placing your orders.

2: Always use a positive form of words

Whatever you order, it must have a positive form of words. Most people seem to have heard of this Rule by now. It's clear why. When, for example, your son says to you you shouldn't fetch his teddy bear for him, then you don't know what you should get him instead. And our experience with children teaches us that everything you bring the child will be wrong, until the child says what he actually wants. The same thing applies to the cosmos. It needs to know what it should get you.

3: Listen to your gut feeling

Your most important task when ordering is to open yourself up to the voice of the cosmic delivery man within you, i.e. to your gut feeling, your intuition, your inner wisdom, the voice of your heart, your inner feeling and so on.

It is pretty rare for the cosmic delivery man to actually ring your doorbell.

Fear, resentment, anger and stress will smother this inner compass, whereas self-love, love, thankfulness, happiness and trust will strengthen it.

This is wonderful. You are probably in the same boat as I am. There is always a lot more potential for development, and while we are working on transforming our fears into trust, resentment into thankfulness and so on, we certainly won't get bored while awaiting our delivery ...

4: You are allowed to make mini-orders too. You can use these to train your ear to hear your inner voice

It is also fine to order little things. People often ask me whether it is all right to pester the cosmos for tiny little things, or if it is better only to order the big things in life. In my experience, our 'connection to up above' acts in a similar way to a muscle. If you never exercise it, it weakens and has to be built up again before you can use it properly.

Little orders help train your ear to listen to your inner voice. In addition, small successes encourage you and put you in a happy frame of mind, and this is exactly the right fundamental frame of mind to have to help the big things to be delivered, too.

5: If you are not sure whether your order is okay, just tack the following words on at the end: '... in a way that serves the best interests of the whole'

What am I allowed to order? If you are not certain, just add the following words at the end of each order: '... in a way that serves the best interests of the whole.' The cosmos is generally far less judgemental than we are. On the other hand, it is the power of universal unity and it is not in the interests of unity if someone tries to take away the free will of others, to manipulate them or get one over on them. The cosmic power of creation certainly won't go along with that. That would be black magic, which is usually associated with sacrifices and dark rituals carried out in a graveyard at night, and things like that.

One of the reasons the cosmos likes to deliver things is that it wants each person to have their own individually happy and fulfilled life. If we are happy, we respect nature and life and see ourselves as their guardians. A person who is in harmony with their self also reflects this in their outward actions.

6: Also ask your heart if it agrees with your order

Which brings us seamlessly to the next point. How do I know if an order is going to be good for me or not? Feel into your heart and imagine that your wish has already come true. How does it make you feel? Is it right or wrong? Ask your heart what it truly desires and what the wish behind the wish is. Wishes founded on self-aggrandisement or fear of what others might think are born of our thoughts, our worries and fears, but certainly not of the wisdom of our hearts.

The interesting thing is the more you practise listening to your heart, so that you don't miss the cosmic delivery man, the more clearly you also hear the voice of your inner esscence, your soul, or whatever you want to call it. And all of a sudden you will find it increasingly easy to differentiate between wishes of the heart and wishes born of fear, and your soul finds it ever easier to tell you its plan.

And a little wrong order from time to time can also be quite helpful. Trial and error can clear up many things that you otherwise might have carried on dreaming of forever. I am thinking, for example, of Johanna from Rule 11. Just to remind you, she wanted to be a child photo model and then found out it was terribly boring. If the cosmos had not delivered her order, this might have remained her wish for many years and she would have been focusing her attention on something that did not suit her at all. This way, she had the experience quickly and could move on.

7: Thankfulness will bring you into the flow of life and open your perception to your inner voice

Practising giving thanks is one of the most important exercises. People who are not thankful and always complain seem to believe that life isn't good enough for them. Just imagine a friend of yours who came over just to whine and whinge and never listened to you for a second. How often would you invite them round?

The exact same thing applies to the cosmos. So relax and enjoy life, even without your order, and practise giving thanks and at the same time listening within yourself. Then the cosmic delivery man will gladly pop by.

Happiness follows the happy because life is alive, and like every live thing it prefers to go to places where the atmophcre is good.

8: Don't tell anyone about your order until it has been delivered, otherwise you put yourself under unnecessary pressure

Don't count your chickens before they hatch. It is a good idea not to tell everyone about your order until it has been delivered. Otherwise everyone will unload their scepticism and doubt on to you, or even make fun of you. This will put you under pressure and you will no longer be able to hear your inner voice.

9: Keep a thought diary. This will help you to keep track of the kind of qualities you usually send the cosmos

We have many thousands of thoughts each day. What is the quality of your thoughts and feelings? What kind of energy do you tend to send out into the cosmos? Try a little experiment. Carry around a little alarm that rings every hour. As soon as you hear the beep, make a note in a small notebook: 'What am I thinking about at the moment? How do I feel right now? Am I judging someone or something at this moment, or am I feeling happy and giving thanks for something? Is there an inner smile on my lips? What is my posture like – upright and stately, or slouching with no energy? What is my level of self-love at the moment?'

If you spend two weeks thinking about these questions every hour (except when you are asleep, of course), you will certainly know very precisely why and how you create things in your life, and how quickly the cosmos is able to deliver!

10: You actually know all of the most important information already. Now is the time to put these things into practice and to start developing your own individual style. Discover your own style and your personal way of communicating with the cosmos

Order Form for Cosmic Ordering

1) The rational mind is the captain of the ship, and it decides the course. Where is the ship going? What do you want to order? Choose a positive form of words.

....

....

....

2) What does your heart say about your order? Is it happy taking part in the order, or is it doing so under protest? There is no stupid or sensible order, no important or unimportant order. Every

order that comes from the heart and is made with joy and strength will open up new opportunities for you. Every order that is made with a muttered protest, or out of pure calculation or fear, will be weak. Ask your heart how much power this order has. Is it really being made from a feeling of happiness and fun?

Start by placing your hand on your heart and listening to its beat for a few minutes. Then ask your heart how it feels about this order, and whether it wants to make any changes.

....

....

....

3) Emotions are your motor, your fuel and your navigation system in one.

Just imagine that your wish has already been fulfilled. How would you feel? Describe this feeling, and in which part of your body you can feel it.

....

....

....

4) This feeling of what it would be like if your order had already been delivered is also 'the wish behind the wish'. We are usually much more interested in receiving the feeling we would like to have than in the actual wish itself. We often only wish for our order because we want to be able to feel a certain way.

a) Order this feeling from the cosmos at the same time:

....

....

....

b) Make a note of the situations in your life that make you feel this way, or in which situations you might be able to experience it easily. Try to experience your wished-for feeling as often as you can in your thoughts or in your daily life, because it will attract everything that matches it – including your current order:

....

....

....

5) The resonance of feeling happy and thankful for life is the resonance of creation. Your intuition and your connection to your inner compass also work best with this fundamental resonance.

a) What can you do so that you feel happy with yourself and your life, just as they are?

....

....

....

b) What are you thankful for?

....

....

....

6) Self-love is the most important thing when cosmic ordering (see the 21 Golden Rules). What sentence would you like to say to yourself today, to turn having a loving attitude towards yourself into a habit?

....

....

....

7) The external observer: just imagine you are a wise old hermit and you meet yourself. You examine your life, your mood and your personal qualities. As a hermit what would you advise yourself to do to be in tune with the cosmos, with yourself and with your inner voice?

....

....

....

Just imagine you are an enlightened child from a different world in which all beings are permanently connected to their godly core. The child lives in a constant state of pure love and joy – and comes to visit you. What would this child advise you to do?

....

....

....

Finally, you can transform yourself in your mind into an old shaman, your favourite wise person, or an enlightened master, an angel, or whatever you prefer. What would this shaman/angel advise you to do to take the next step towards achieving your highest potential in life?

8) Once a week, check for coincidences, signs and your emotional navigation system: you have made your order. What has happened since then? Have there been any coincidences or signs? Have new opportunities come along? Has your heart told you to follow any specific path, to do a certain thing or talk to a specific person? How

well did exercises 4b to 7 go for you? Has your order already been delivered? Give thanks to the cosmos and yourself for every order that is delivered. Congratulate yourself and consciously enjoy every moment of your life – with or without your delivery.

....

....

....

9) Opposition and resentment will increase the thing you are fighting against. Just imagine that everything is already happening in your best interest. By learning to do what you need to reconcile yourself, you are preparing the way to receive the coming changes and deliveries.

Your life is a miracle and you are a winner – no matter what happens. After all, didn't you win a race with millions of other sperm cells at your conception? You were the fastest one to the egg. And you became a person. This alone makes you a winner and you should celebrate every second of your life. The other couple of million are still waiting in the wings, you are already here! Congratulate yourself and be happy!

Make a list of all of the wonderful things you have already experienced in your life. Giving thanks for the wonderful things will pull more wonderful things into your life, strengthen your intuition and your inner compass.

....

....

....

10) Well, if I have to fill out such a long list just for one order, then I might as well send off another nice little order along with it, just for fun. Just so that the cosmos knows that I enjoy being in contact with it, and to exercise my 'happiness-in-ordering muscle.'

Here is my extra order:

....

....

....

Express Order Form

Dear Cosmos,

I would like to order:

....

This is what I do to keep my intuition in tune:

....

I love myself just the way I am, and also tell myself this:

....

This is my wished-for feeling, which I would also like to order:

....

Thank you, thank you, thank you!

Finished ☺

Dear Cosmos,

I would like to order:

....

This is what I do to keep my intuition in tune:

....

I love myself just the way I am, and also tell myself this:

....

This is my wished-for feeling, which I would also like to order:

....

Thank you, thank you, thank you!

Finished ☺

Dear Cosmos,

I would like to order:

....

This is what I do to keep my intuition in tune:

....

I love myself just the way I am, and also tell myself this:

....

This is my wished-for feeling, which I would also like to order:

....

Thank you, thank you, thank you!

Finished ☺

Dear Cosmos,

I would like to order:

....

This is what I do to keep my intuition in tune:

....

I love myself just the way I am, and also tell myself this:

....

This is my wished-for feeling, which I would also like to order:

....

Thank you, thank you, thank you!

Finished ☺

Further Reading

For Rule 4

Joachim Bauer: *Warum ich fühle, was du fühlst* [*Why I Feel What You Feel: Intuitive Communication and the Secret of Mirror Neurons*], Heyne Verlag, 2005

For Rule 8

Masaru Emoto: *The Hidden Messages in Water*, Pocket Books, 2005

Alexander Lauterwasser: *Water Sound Images: The Creative Music of the Universe*, MACROmedia Publishing, 2007

For Rules 11 and 12

For a feeling of increased inner fulfilment for wealthy people:

Barbel Mohr: *The Millionaires' Shopping Guide for Greater Inner Wealth* (free e-book download), www.baerbelmohr.de/english-version/books, 2008

For unemployed people:

Bärbel Mohr und Laila Schmid: *Arbeitslos und trotzdem glücklich* [*Unemployed and Happy Nonetheless*], KOHA Verlag, 2009

For Rule 17

Barbel Mohr: *Cosmic Ordering: The Next Step*, Hay House, 2009

Barbara Sher and Barbara Smith: *I Could Do Anything If I Only Knew What It Was: How to Discover What You Really Want and How to Get It*, Bantam Doubleday Dell Publishing Group, 1994

Pierre Franckh: *Das Gesetz der Resonanz* [*The Law of Resonance*], KOHA Verlag, 2008

For Rule 19

Barbara Sher and Annie Gottlieb: *Wishcraft: How to Get What You Really Want*, Ballantine Books, 2003

For Rule 20

Marshall Rosenberg: *Non-violent Communication: A Language of Life*, Puddle Dancer Press, 2003

Also Available
by Barbel Mohr

Note: the Golden Rules summarise the best out of all of these books.

Cosmic Ordering for Beginners (Hay House, 2010)

Cosmic Ordering: The Next Adventure (Hodder Mobius, 2007)

Cosmic Ordering: The Next Step (Hay House, 2009)

Cosmic Ordering Oracle Cards (Hay House, 2007)

The Cosmic Ordering Service (Hodder Mobius, 2006)

Cosmic Ordering: Why It Works DVD (Hay House, 2009)

The Cosmic Ordering Wish Book 2010 (Hay House, 2009)

Instant Cosmic Ordering (Hay House, 2008)

About the Author

Barbel's first and most successful book, *The Cosmic Ordering Service*, introduced Cosmic Ordering to the world. Barbel wrote more than 20 books on a variety of subjects, and sold over a million books on Cosmic Ordering alone. Her books enjoyed great success in the UK after Noel Edmonds said that he used Cosmic Ordering to order a TV comeback, a new partner and a new house.

Barbel travelled all over the world teaching transformational workshops on Cosmic Ordering until her death in 2010.

www.baerbelmohr.de – for books, tips, info and shop.

www.baerbelmohrblog.de – a webzine with readers' comments.

www.cosmic-ordering.de – dedicated to the 'hopping' technique.

NOTES

NOTES

NOTES

NOTES

NOTES

NOTES

NOTES

Hay House Titles of Related Interest

We hope you enjoyed this Hay House book.
If you would like to receive a free catalogue featuring additional
Hay House books and products, or if you would like information
about the Hay Foundation, please contact:

Hay House UK Ltd
292B Kensal Road • London W10 5BE
Tel: (44) 20 8962 1230; Fax: (44) 20 8962 1239
www.hayhouse.co.uk

***

Published and distributed in the United States of America by:
Hay House, Inc. • PO Box 5100 • Carlsbad, CA 92018-5100
Tel: (1) 760 431 7695 or (1) 800 654 5126;
Fax: (1) 760 431 6948 or (1) 800 650 5115
www.hayhouse.com

***

Published and distributed in Australia by:
Hay House Australia Ltd • 18/36 Ralph Street • Alexandria, NSW 2015
Tel: (61) 2 9669 4299, Fax: (61) 2 9669 4144
www.hayhouse.com.au

***

Published and distributed in the Republic of South Africa by:
Hay House SA (Pty) Ltd • PO Box 990 • Witkoppen 2068
Tel/Fax: (27) 11 467 8904
www.hayhouse.co.za

***

Published and distributed in India by:
Hay House Publishers India • Muskaan Complex • Plot No.3
B-2 • Vasant Kunj • New Delhi - 110 070
Tel: (91) 11 41761620; Fax: (91) 11 41761630
www.hayhouse.co.in

***

Distributed in Canada by:
Raincoast • 9050 Shaughnessy St • Vancouver, BC V6P 6E5
Tel: (1) 604 323 7100
Fax: (1) 604 323 2600

***

Sign up via the Hay House UK website to receive the Hay House
online newsletter and stay informed about what's going on with your
favourite authors. You'll receive bimonthly announcements
about discounts and offers, special events, product highlights,
free excerpts, giveaways, and more!
www.hayhouse.co.uk